TABLE OF CONTENTS

Chapter 1

Chapter 2

Chapter 3

Chapter 4

Chapter 5

Chapter 6

Chapter 7

Chapter 8

Chapter 9

Chapter 10

C# ESSENTIALS

FROM BEGINNER TO PRO

OLIVER LUCAS JR

PREFACE

Welcome to the world of C#, a versatile and powerful programming language that has revolutionized software development. Whether you're a seasoned developer or just starting your coding journey, this book is designed to equip you with the essential knowledge and skills to master C#.

Throughout this book, you'll embark on a comprehensive exploration of C# concepts, from the fundamentals of syntax and data types to advanced topics like asynchronous programming and parallel processing. We'll guide you through practical examples, hands-on exercises, and real-world scenarios to solidify your understanding.

By the end of this book, you'll be able to:

Write clean, efficient, and maintainable C# code.

Leverage the power of object-oriented programming.

Utilize advanced language features like LINQ and generics.

Build robust and scalable applications.

Explore the .NET ecosystem and its various frameworks.

This book is your companion on your C# learning journey. Let's dive in and unlock the full potential of this remarkable language!

Chapter 1

Introduction to C#

1.1 A Brief History of C#

C# (pronounced "C sharp") is a modern, object-oriented programming language developed by Microsoft. It was first released in 2000 as part of the .NET[1] Framework.

Key Points in C#'s History:

Early Development: C# was designed to be a simple, modern, general-purpose language that could be used for a variety of applications. It drew inspiration from languages like C++, Java, and Delphi.

.NET Framework Integration: C# was closely tied to the .NET Framework, a software framework that provides a consistent programming model across different platforms. This integration allowed C# to leverage the power of the .NET Framework's libraries and tools.

Evolution and Standardization: Over the years, C# has evolved through various versions, adding new features and improving performance. It has also been standardized by the ECMA and ISO/IEC, ensuring its widespread adoption and compatibility.

Open-Source and Cross-Platform: With the rise of open-source development, C# has become increasingly cross-platform. The .NET Core framework allows C# applications to run on Windows, macOS, and Linux.

Modern Language Features: C# has embraced modern language features like LINQ, asynchronous programming, and functional programming paradigms, making it a powerful and versatile language for contemporary software development.

C#'s versatility and strong community support have contributed to its popularity among developers. It is used in a wide range of applications, from desktop software to web development, game development, and mobile app development.

1.2 Setting Up Your C# Development Environment

1. Install Visual Studio:

Download: Visit the official Visual Studio website and download the latest version.

Installation: Follow the on-screen instructions to install Visual Studio. Ensure you select the **.NET desktop development** workload during installation.

2. Create a New C# Project:

Open Visual Studio: Launch the installed Visual Studio.

Create a New Project:

Click on **Create a new project**.

Choose a template like **Console App (.NET Framework)** or **Console App (.NET Core)**.

Give your project a name and choose a location.

Click **Create**.

3. Write Your First C# Code:

Open the `Program.cs` file: This is where you'll write your C# code.

Write a simple "Hello, World!" program:

C#

```
using System;

namespace HelloWorld
{
    class Program
    {
        static void Main(string[] args)
        {
            Console.WriteLine("Hello, World!");[1]
        }
    }
}
```

4. Run the Program:

Press F5: This will build and run your program.

Check the Output: The "Hello, World!" message will be displayed in the console window.

Additional Tips:

.NET Core: Consider using .NET Core for cross-platform development. It's a lightweight and modular framework.

Visual Studio Code: A lightweight, open-source code editor that can be used with C# and .NET Core.

Online IDEs: For quick prototyping, you can use online IDEs like Replit or CodePen.

C# Tutorials: Explore online tutorials and courses to learn C# concepts in depth.

By following these steps, you'll have a solid foundation to start your C# programming journey.

1.3 Your First C# Program

Your First C# Program: "Hello, World!"

Let's break down the "Hello, World!" program we discussed earlier:

C#

```
using System;

namespace HelloWorld
{
    class Program
    {
        static void Main(string[] args)
        {
            Console.WriteLine("Hello, World!");
        }
    }
}
```

Understanding[1] the Code:

`using System;`:

This line tells the compiler to import the `System` namespace.

The `System` namespace contains fundamental classes and functionalities, including the `Console` class.

`namespace HelloWorld`:

This line declares a namespace named `HelloWorld`.

A namespace is a way to organize code into logical units.

`class Program`:

This line declares a class named `Program`.

A class is a blueprint for creating objects.

`static void Main(string[] args)`:

This line defines the `Main` method, the entry point of the program.

`static`: This keyword indicates that the method belongs to the class itself, not to an instance of the class.

`void`: This keyword indicates that the method doesn't return any value.

`Main`: This is the name of the method.

`string[] args`: This parameter is an array of strings that can be used to pass arguments to the program when it's executed from the command line.

`Console.WriteLine("Hello, World!");`:

This line writes the string "Hello, World!" to the console.

`Console.WriteLine`: This method is used to write output to the console.

Running the Program:

Compile: The compiler translates the C# code into machine-readable instructions.

Execute: The compiled program is executed, and the "Hello, World!" message is displayed in the console.

Experimenting Further:

Modify the message: Change the text inside the `Console.WriteLine` method to display a different message.

Add more lines: Write multiple `Console.WriteLine` statements to display multiple lines of text.

Use variables: Declare variables to store data and manipulate them within the program.

By understanding this basic program, you've taken the first step towards mastering C#. Let's continue building upon this foundation!

Chapter 2

C# Basics

2.1 Variables, Data Types, and Operators

Variables, Data Types, and Operators in C#

Variables

A variable is a named storage location that holds a value. In C#, you declare a variable by specifying its data type and name:

C#

```
data_type variable_name;
```

Example:

C#

```
int age = 25;
string name = "Alice";
double pi = 3.14159;
```

Data Types

Data types define the kind of data a variable can hold. Here are some common data types in C#:

Primitive Data Types:

`int`: Integer numbers (e.g., 42, -10)

`float`: Single-precision floating-point numbers (e.g., 3.14f)

`double`: Double-precision floating-point numbers (e.g., 3.14159)

`char`: Single character (e.g., 'A', 'b')

`bool`: Boolean value (true or false)

`string`: Sequence of characters (e.g., "Hello, World!")

Reference Data Types:

`string`: Represents a sequence of characters.

`array`: A collection of elements of the same data type.

`class`: A blueprint for creating objects.

Operators

Operators are symbols used to perform operations on variables and values.

Arithmetic Operators:

`+`: Addition

`-`: Subtraction

`*`: Multiplication

`/`: Division

`%`: Modulus[1] (remainder)

Comparison Operators:

`==`: Equal to

`!=`: Not equal to

>: Greater than

<: Less than

>=: Greater than or equal to

<=: Less than or equal to

Logical Operators:[2]

&&: Logical AND

||: Logical OR

!: Logical NOT[3]

Example:

C#

```
int x = 10;
int y = 5;

int sum = x + y;
int difference = x - y;
int product = x * y;
int quotient = x / y;
int remainder = x % y;

bool isGreater = x > y;
bool isEqual = x == y;

Console.WriteLine("Sum: " + sum);
Console.WriteLine("Difference: " + difference);
Console.WriteLine("Product: " + product);
Console.WriteLine("Quotient: " + quotient);
Console.WriteLine("Remainder:[4] " + remainder);
Console.WriteLine("Is x greater than y? " + isGreater);
Console.WriteLine("Is x equal to y? " + isEqual);
```

2.2 Control Flow Statements

Control Flow Statements in C#

Control flow statements allow you to control the order in which your code executes. Here are the primary control flow statements in C#:

1. Conditional Statements

if Statement:

Executes a block of code if a condition is true.

C#

```
if (condition)
{
    // Code to execute if condition is true
}
```

if-else Statement:

Executes one block of code if a condition is true, and another block if it's false.

C#

```
if (condition)
{
    // Code to execute if condition is true
}
else
{
```

```
    // Code to execute if condition is false
}
```

if-else-if Ladder:

Allows you to check multiple conditions.

C#

```
if (condition1)
{
    // Code to execute if condition1 is true
}
else if (condition2)
{
    // Code to execute if condition1 is false and condition2[1] is true
}
else
{
    // Code to execute if both conditions[2] are false
}
```

2. Looping Statements

for Loop:

Executes a block of code a specific number of times.

C#

```
for (initialization; condition; increment/decrement)
{
    // Code to execute
}
```

while Loop:

Executes a block of code repeatedly as long as a condition is true.

C#

```
while (condition)
{
    // Code to execute
}
```

do-while Loop:

Executes a block of code at least once, and then repeatedly as long as a condition is true.

C#

```
do
{
    // Code to execute
} while (condition);
```

Example:

C#

```
int number = 10;

if (number > 0)
{
    Console.WriteLine("The number is positive.");
}
else
{
     Console.WriteLine("The number is negative or
zero.");
}

for (int i = 1; i <= 5; i++)
{
    Console.WriteLine("Iteration: " + i);
}

int count = 1;
while (count <= 3)
{
    Console.WriteLine("Count: " + count);
    count++;
}

int j = 1;
do
{
    Console.WriteLine("Do-while loop: " + j);
    j++;
} while (j <= 2);
```

Chapter 3

Object-Oriented Programming (OOP)

3.1 Classes, Objects, and Inheritance

Classes

A class is a blueprint for creating objects. It defines the properties and methods that objects of that class will have.

Example:

C#

```
public class Car
{
    public string Color { get; set; }
    public int Year { get; set; }

    public void Start()
    {
        Console.WriteLine("Car started.");
    }

    public void Stop()
    {
        Console.WriteLine("Car stopped.");
    }
}
```

Objects

An object is an instance of a class. It has its own unique set of properties and can perform the methods defined in the class.

Example:

C#

```
Car myCar = new Car();
myCar.Color = "Red";
myCar.Year = 2023;
myCar.Start();
```

Inheritance

Inheritance is a mechanism that allows one class to inherit the properties and methods of another class. The class that inherits[1] is called the derived class or subclass, and the class being inherited from is called the base class or superclass.[2]

Example:

C#

```
public class Vehicle
{
    public string Color { get; set; }
    public int Year { get; set; }

    public void Start()
    {
        Console.WriteLine("Vehicle started.");
    }

    public void Stop()
```

```
    {
        Console.WriteLine("Vehicle stopped.");
    }
}

public class Car : Vehicle
{
    public int Horsepower { get; set; }
}
```

In this example, the `Car` class inherits from the `Vehicle` class. This means that `Car` objects have all the properties and methods of `Vehicle` objects, plus the additional `Horsepower` property.

Key Points:

Encapsulation: Wrapping data and methods within a class to protect data integrity.

Polymorphism: The ability of objects of different types to be treated as objects of a common superclass.

Abstraction: Hiding implementation details and exposing only the necessary interface.

By understanding classes, objects, and inheritance, you can create well-structured and reusable C# code.

3.2 Polymorphism and Encapsulation

Polymorphism

Polymorphism is the ability of objects of different types to be treated as objects of a common superclass. This allows you to write more flexible and reusable code.

Types of Polymorphism:

Compile-time Polymorphism (Method Overloading):

Different methods with the same name but different parameters.

The compiler determines which method to call based on the arguments[1] passed.

C#

```
public class Calculator
{
    public int Add(int a, int b)
    {
        return a + b;
    }

    public double Add(double a, double b)
    {
        return a + b;
    }
}
```

Runtime Polymorphism (Method Overriding):[2]

A derived class overrides a method inherited from a base class.

The specific implementation of the method is determined at runtime based on the object's actual type.

C#

```
public class Animal
{
    public virtual void MakeSound()
    {
                    Console.WriteLine("Generic  animal
sound");
    }
}

public class Dog : Animal
{
    public override void MakeSound()
    {
        Console.WriteLine("Woof!");3
    }
}
```

Encapsulation

Encapsulation is the process of hiding the implementation details of an object and exposing only the necessary[4] interface. This helps to protect the internal state of an object and promotes modularity.

Key Principles of Encapsulation:

Data Hiding:

Declaring class members as private to restrict direct access.

Providing public methods (getters and setters) to control access to private members.

Information Hiding:

Exposing only the necessary information to the outside world.

Hiding implementation details to make the code more maintainable and less prone to errors.

Example:

C#

```
public class Person
{
    private string name;
    private int age;

    public string Name
    {
        get { return name; }
        set { name = value; }
    }

    public int Age
    {
        get { return age;[5] }
        set { age = value;[6] }
    }
}
```

In this example, the `name` and `age` fields are private, and their values can only be accessed and modified through the public `Name` and `Age` properties. This ensures that the internal state of the `Person` object is protected and can only be changed in a controlled manner.

By understanding and applying polymorphism and encapsulation, you can create more flexible, maintainable, and reusable C# code.

Chapter 4

Arrays, Collections, and Strings

4.1 Arrays and Lists

Arrays

An array is a collection of elements of the same data type, stored in contiguous memory locations.

Declaration:

C#

```
data_type[] array_name = new data_type[size];
```

Example:

C#

```
int[] numbers = new int[5];
```

Accessing Elements:

C#

```
numbers[0] = 10;
numbers[1] = 20;
// ...
```

Lists

A List is a dynamic collection of objects, which can grow or shrink in size as needed. It provides more flexibility than arrays.

Declaration:

C#

```
List<data_type> list_name = new List<data_type>();
```

Example:

C#

```
List<string> names = new List<string>();
names.Add("Alice");
names.Add("Bob");
names.Add("Charlie");
```

Common List Operations:

Add: Adds an element to the end of the list.

Remove: Removes an element from the list.

RemoveAt: Removes an element at a specific index.

Clear: Removes all elements from the list.

Count: Returns the number of elements in the list.

Contains: Checks if an element exists in the list.

IndexOf: Returns the index of the first occurrence of an element.

Sort: Sorts the elements in the list.

Example:

C#

```
Console.WriteLine("List of names:");
foreach (string name in names)
{
    Console.WriteLine(name);
}
```

Key Differences Between Arrays and Lists:

Feature	Arrays	Lists
Fixed size	Yes	No
Data type	Must be the same for all elements	Can hold elements of the same data type
Accessing elements	Using index	Using index or methods like `ElementAt`

Choose the right data structure based on your specific needs:

Arrays: Use when you know the exact size of the collection beforehand and performance is critical.

Lists: Use when you need a dynamic collection that can grow or shrink, or when you need to perform frequent insertions, deletions, or searches.

4.2 Dictionaries and Sets

Dictionaries and Sets in C#

Dictionaries

A dictionary is a collection of key-value pairs. It allows you to efficiently store and retrieve values based on their associated keys.

Declaration:

C#

```
Dictionary<key_type, value_type> dictionary_name = new Dictionary<key_type, value_type>();
```

Example:

C#

```
Dictionary<string, int> ages = new Dictionary<string, int>();
ages.Add("Alice", 25);
ages.Add("Bob", 30);
ages.Add("Charlie", 28);

Console.WriteLine(ages["Alice"]); // Output: 25
```

Key Operations:

Add: Adds a key-value pair to the dictionary.

Remove: Removes a key-value pair from the dictionary.

ContainsKey: Checks if a key exists in the dictionary.

TryGetValue: Retrieves a value associated with a key, returning a boolean indicating success.

Clear: Removes all key-value pairs from the dictionary.

Count: Returns the number of key-value pairs in the dictionary.

Sets

A set is a collection of unique elements. It doesn't allow duplicate values.

Declaration:

C#

```
HashSet<data_type> set_name = new
HashSet<data_type>();
```

Example:

C#

```
HashSet<int> numbers = new HashSet<int>();
numbers.Add(10);
numbers.Add(20);
numbers.Add(10); // Duplicate, won't be added

Console.WriteLine(numbers.Count); // Output: 2
```

Key Operations:

Add: Adds an element to the set.

Remove: Removes an element from the set.

Contains: Checks if an element exists in the set.

Clear: Removes all elements from the set.

Count: Returns the number of elements in the set.

Choosing Between Dictionaries and Sets:

Dictionaries: Use when you need to associate values with unique keys.

Sets: Use when you need to store unique elements without any specific key-value association.

By understanding dictionaries and sets, you can efficiently manage and manipulate data in your C# applications.

4.3 String Manipulation

Strings are sequences of characters enclosed in double quotes. C# provides a rich set of methods to manipulate strings.

Basic Operations:

Concatenation: Combining strings using the + operator or the `Concat` method.

C#

```
string firstName = "Alice";
string lastName = "Johnson";
string fullName = firstName + " " + lastName;
string fullName2 = string.Concat(firstName, " ", lastName);
```

Length: Getting the length of a string.

C#

```
int length = fullName.Length;
```

Indexing: Accessing individual characters using index.

C#

```
char firstChar = fullName[0];
```

Substring: Extracting a portion of a string.

C#

```
string lastNameOnly = fullName.Substring(6);
```

Common String Methods:

ToLower: Converts all characters to lowercase.

ToUpper: Converts all characters to uppercase.

Trim: Removes leading and trailing whitespace.

TrimStart: Removes leading whitespace.

TrimEnd: Removes trailing whitespace.

Replace: Replaces occurrences of one substring with another.

Split: Splits a string into a string array based on a delimiter.

Join: Joins elements of an array or collection into a string.

Example:

C#

```
string text = "Hello, World!";

// Convert to uppercase
```

```
string upperText = text.ToUpper();

// Replace "World" with "C#"
string newText = text.Replace("World", "C#");

// Split the string into words
string[] words = text.Split(' ');

// Join the words with a hyphen
string hyphenatedText = string.Join("-", words);

Console.WriteLine(upperText);
Console.WriteLine(newText);
Console.WriteLine(hyphenatedText);
```

Regular Expressions: Regular expressions provide a powerful way to pattern-match and manipulate text.

C#

```
string pattern = @"^\d{3}-\d{3}-\d{4}$";
string phoneNumber = "123-456-7890";

bool isValid = Regex.IsMatch(phoneNumber, pattern);
```

By mastering string manipulation techniques, you can effectively process and transform text data in your C# applications.

Chapter 5

Exception Handling and File I/O

5.1 Try-Catch-Finally Blocks

Try-catch-finally blocks are used to handle exceptions, which are errors that occur during program execution. This mechanism helps to prevent program crashes and provides a way to gracefully handle errors.

Try Block

The `try` block encloses the code that might throw an exception.

Catch Block

The `catch` block handles the exception if it occurs. Multiple catch blocks can be used to handle different types of exceptions.[1]

Finally Block

The `finally` block is optional. It always executes, regardless of whether an exception is thrown or not. It's often used for cleanup tasks like closing files or releasing resources.

Example:

C#

```
int[] numbers = { 10, 20, 0 };

try
{
    int result = 100 / numbers[2];
```

```
    Console.WriteLine(result);
}
catch (DivideByZeroException ex)
{
        Console.WriteLine("Error: Division by zero.");
    Console.WriteLine(ex.Message);
}
finally
{
        Console.WriteLine("This will always execute.");
}
```

In this example:

The `try` block attempts to divide 100 by `numbers[2]`, which is 0.

This causes a `DivideByZeroException`.

The `catch` block handles the exception, prints an error message, and the exception message.

The `finally` block executes, printing "This will always execute."

Custom Exceptions:

You can create your own custom exceptions by deriving from the `Exception` class.

C#

```
public class NegativeNumberException : Exception
```

```
{
            public   NegativeNumberException(string
message) : base(message) { }
}
```

Best Practices:

Use specific exception types to catch and handle different errors.

Provide informative error messages.

Use `finally` blocks to release resources, even if an exception occurs.

Avoid empty `catch` blocks.

Log exceptions for debugging and troubleshooting.

By effectively using try-catch-finally blocks, you can write more robust and error-resistant C# applications.

5.2 Reading and Writing Files

C# provides several ways to read from and write to files. Here are two common methods:

1. Using `System.IO` Namespace

Reading a Text File:

C#

```
using System.IO;

string filePath = "data.txt";

try
{
    string[] lines = File.ReadAllLines(filePath);
    foreach (string line in lines)
    {
        Console.WriteLine(line);
    }
}
catch (IOException ex)
{
      Console.WriteLine("Error reading file: " +
ex.Message);
}
```

Writing to a Text File:

C#

```
using System.IO;

string filePath = "output.txt";

try
{
    File.WriteAllText(filePath, "Hello, world!");
    File.AppendAllText(filePath, "\nThis is a new
line.");
}
catch (IOException ex)
{
```

```
    Console.WriteLine("Error writing to file: " +
ex.Message);
}
```

2. Using StreamReader and StreamWriter

Reading a Text File:

C#

```
using System.IO;

string filePath = "data.txt";

try
{
    using (StreamReader reader = new
StreamReader(filePath))
    {
        string line;
        while ((line = reader.ReadLine()) !=
null)
        {
            Console.WriteLine(line);
        }
    }
}
catch (IOException1 ex)
{
    Console.WriteLine("Error reading file: " +
ex.Message);
}
```

Writing to a Text File:

C#

```
using System.IO;

string filePath = "output.txt";

try
{
    using (StreamWriter writer = new StreamWriter(filePath))
    {
        writer.WriteLine("Hello, world!");
        writer.WriteLine("This is a new line.");
    }
}
catch (IOException ex)
{
    Console.WriteLine("Error writing to file: " + ex.Message);
}
```

Key Points:

Error Handling: Always use `try-catch` blocks to handle potential exceptions like file not found, access denied, or disk errors.

File Paths: Ensure correct file paths, especially when working with relative and absolute paths.

Closing Files: Use the `using` statement to automatically close file streams, preventing resource leaks.

File Modes: You can specify different file modes (e.g., `FileMode.Create`, `FileMode.Append`) when creating or opening files.

Text vs. Binary: For binary files, use `FileStream` and `BinaryReader`/`BinaryWriter`.

Performance: Consider using buffered I/O operations for large files to improve performance.

By understanding these concepts and best practices, you can effectively read from and write to files in your C# applications.

Chapter 6

LINQ and Generics

6.1 Language Integrated Query (LINQ)

Language Integrated Query (LINQ)

LINQ (Language Integrated Query) is a powerful feature in C# that allows you to query and manipulate data sources in a unified way, using a syntax similar to SQL. LINQ provides a consistent way to work with various data sources, including arrays, lists, collections, databases, and XML documents.

Basic LINQ Query Structure:

C#

```
var query = from element in source
            where condition
            select element;
```

Example:

C#

```
int[] numbers = { 1, 2, 3, 4, 5 };

// Query for even numbers
var evenNumbers = from num in numbers
                  where num % 2 == 0
                  select num;
```

```
// Iterate over the results
foreach (int number in evenNumbers)
{
    Console.WriteLine(number);
}
```

LINQ Methods:

LINQ also provides a method-based syntax, which is often more concise and flexible:

C#

```
var evenNumbers = numbers.Where(num => num %
2 == 0);
```

Common LINQ Methods:

Where: Filters elements based on a condition.

Select: Projects each element to a new form.

OrderBy: Sorts elements in ascending order.

OrderByDescending: Sorts elements in descending order.

FirstOrDefault: Returns the first element or a default value.

LastOrDefault: Returns the last element or a default value.

Any: Checks if any element matches a condition.

All: Checks if all elements match a condition.

Count: Counts the number of elements.

Sum: Calculates the sum of numeric values.

Average: Calculates the average of numeric values.

Max: Returns the maximum value.

Min: Returns the minimum value.

LINQ to Objects:

LINQ to Objects allows you to query in-memory collections like arrays and lists.

LINQ to SQL:

LINQ to SQL enables you to query databases using a LINQ-like syntax.

LINQ to XML:

LINQ to XML provides a fluent API for working with XML documents.

Key Benefits of LINQ:

Unified Query Syntax: A consistent way to query different data sources.

Improved Readability: LINQ queries are often more readable than traditional loops and conditional statements.

Increased Productivity: LINQ can significantly reduce the amount of code required to perform complex data operations.

Powerful Query Capabilities: LINQ offers a wide range of operators for filtering, sorting, grouping, and projecting data.

By mastering LINQ, you can write more efficient and expressive C# code.

6.2 Generic Classes and Methods

Generic classes and methods allow you to write reusable code that can work with different data types. This promotes type safety and code flexibility.

Generic Classes

A generic class is defined using angle brackets `<>` and a placeholder type parameter.

C#

```
public class GenericClass<T>
{
    private T data;

    public void SetData(T value)
    {
        data = value;
    }

    public T GetData()
    {
        return data;
    }
}
```

In this example, `T` is a type parameter. When you create an instance of `GenericClass`, you specify the actual type:

C#

```
GenericClass<int> intClass = new GenericClass<int>();

intClass.SetData(42);


GenericClass<string> stringClass = new GenericClass<string>();

stringClass.SetData("Hello");
```

Generic Methods

A generic method is a method that can work with different data types.

C#

```
public static T GetMax<T>(T a, T b) where T : IComparable<T>

{

    if (a.CompareTo(b) > 0)

    {

        return a;

    }

    else

    {

        return b;

    }

}
```

In this example, the `where T : IComparable<T>` constraint ensures that the `T` type must implement the `IComparable<T>` interface, which allows objects of that type to be compared.

Key Points:

Generic classes and methods promote code reusability and type safety.

Type parameters can be used to define generic interfaces and delegates.

Generic constraints can be used to restrict the types that can be used with a generic class or method.

Consider using generic types when you need to write code that can work with different data types.

By understanding and using generic classes and methods, you can write more flexible and efficient C# code.

Chapter 7

Asynchronous Programming and Parallelism

7.1 Async/Await Keywords

Asynchronous programming is a programming paradigm that allows you to perform long-running tasks without blocking the main thread of execution. This enables your application to remain responsive and avoid freezing.

C# provides the `async` and `await` keywords to simplify asynchronous programming.

`async` Keyword

Marks a method as asynchronous.

Indicates that the method may contain asynchronous operations.

Returns a `Task` or `Task<T>` object.

`await` Keyword

Used within an `async` method to pause execution until an asynchronous operation completes.

The result of the asynchronous operation is returned.

Example:

C#

```
async Task DownloadFileAsync(string url)
{
```

```
            using (HttpClient client = new HttpClient())
        {
            byte[] data = await client.GetByteArrayAsync(url);
            // Process the downloaded data
        }
    }
```

How it works:

When the await keyword is encountered, the current method pauses execution.

The asynchronous operation (in this case, client.GetByteArrayAsync) continues to run in the background.

The method resumes execution when the asynchronous operation completes, and the result is assigned to the data variable.

Key Points:

async methods must be marked with the async keyword.

await can only be used within async methods.

await can only be used on expressions that return a Task or Task<T>.

async methods typically return a Task or Task<T>.

Best Practices:

Use `async` and `await` for I/O-bound operations like network requests, file I/O, and database access.

Avoid using `async` and `await` for CPU-bound operations, as they may not provide significant performance benefits.

Handle exceptions appropriately using `try-catch` blocks.

Consider using `async` and `await` in a consistent manner throughout your application.

By effectively using `async` and `await`, you can write more responsive and efficient C# applications.

7.2 Task Parallel Library (TPL)

Task Parallel Library (TPL)

The Task Parallel Library (TPL) is a powerful library in the .NET Framework that simplifies parallel programming. It allows you to easily write asynchronous and parallel code without managing threads directly.

Key Concepts:

Task: Represents a single unit of work.

Task Parallelism: Multiple tasks are executed concurrently on different threads.

Data Parallelism: The same operation is performed on multiple data items concurrently.

Using TPL:

Create Tasks:

C#

```
Task task1 = Task.Run(() =>
{
    // Task 1's work
});

Task task2 = Task.Factory.StartNew(() =>
{
    // Task 2's work
});
```

Wait for Tasks to Complete:

C#

```
Task.WaitAll(task1, task2);
```

Get Task Results:

C#

```
int result = task1.Result;
```

Parallel For Loop:

C#

```
Parallel.For(0, 10, i =>
{
    // Process each number in parallel
});
```

Parallel ForEach:

C#

```
Parallel.ForEach(numbers, number =>
{
    // Process each number in parallel
});
```

Important Considerations:

Thread Safety: Ensure that your code is thread-safe when accessing shared resources.

Task Scheduling: The TPL automatically schedules tasks to available threads.

Exception Handling: Use appropriate techniques to handle exceptions that may occur in parallel tasks.

Performance: Consider the overhead of creating and managing tasks, especially for small tasks.

Cancellation: Use cancellation tokens to cancel running tasks.

Example: Parallel Downloading

C#

```
async Task DownloadFilesAsync(IEnumerable<string> urls)
{
    var downloadTasks = urls.Select(url => DownloadFileAsync(url));
    await Task.WhenAll(downloadTasks);
}

async Task<byte[]> DownloadFileAsync(string url)
{
    using (HttpClient client = new HttpClient())
    {
        return await client.GetByteArrayAsync(url);
```

```
        }
    }
```

By using TPL, you can significantly improve the performance and responsiveness of your applications, especially when dealing with CPU-bound or I/O-bound tasks.

Chapter 8

C# and .NET Framework

8.1 .NET Framework Overview

.NET Framework Overview

The .NET Framework is a software framework developed by Microsoft that provides a programming environment for building various applications, including Windows desktop applications, web applications, and web services.

Key Components of the .NET Framework:

Common Language Runtime (CLR):

Manages the execution of .NET applications.

Provides memory management, garbage collection, and security features.

Ensures type safety and code verification.

Base Class Library (BCL):

A collection of reusable classes, interfaces, and value types that provide basic functionality.

Includes classes for file I/O, network communication, string manipulation, and more.

Framework Class Library (FCL):

A set of libraries that extend the functionality of the BCL.

Includes libraries for Windows Forms, ASP.NET, ADO.NET, and WPF.

Core Features of the .NET Framework:

Language Independence: Supports multiple programming languages like C#, Visual Basic .NET, and F#.

Common Language Runtime (CLR): A managed execution environment that provides memory management and security.

Base Class Library (BCL): A rich collection of reusable classes for common tasks.

Windows Forms: A framework for building Windows desktop applications.

ASP.NET: A framework for building web applications and services.

ADO.NET: A framework for data access and manipulation.

Windows Presentation Foundation (WPF): A framework for building rich user interfaces.

Windows Communication Foundation (WCF): A framework for building service-oriented applications.

.NET Framework vs. .NET Core:

While the .NET Framework is a full-featured framework for Windows development, .NET Core is a cross-platform, open-source framework that can run on Windows, macOS, and Linux. .NET Core offers a modular design, improved performance, and a smaller footprint.

Conclusion:

The .NET Framework provides a powerful and versatile platform for building a wide range of applications. Its strong foundation, rich feature set, and large developer community make it a popular choice for many developers.

8.2 Windows Forms and WPF

Windows Forms and WPF

Windows Forms

Windows Forms is a framework for building Windows desktop applications. It provides a rich set of controls, such as buttons, text boxes, and data grids, to create user interfaces.

Key Features:

Easy to learn and use.

Drag-and-drop interface design.

Event-driven programming model.

Supports a wide range of controls.

Example:

C#

```
using System;

using System.Windows.Forms;


namespace WindowsFormsApp

{

    public partial class Form1 : Form

    {

        public Form1()

        {

            InitializeComponent();

        }
```

```
        private void button1_Click(object[1]
sender, EventArgs e)
        {
                MessageBox.Show("Hello,
World!");
        }
    }
}
```

Windows[2] Presentation Foundation (WPF)

WPF is a more advanced framework for building rich user interfaces. It offers a flexible and powerful way to create visually stunning applications.

Key Features:

XAML-based declarative UI design.

Data binding and templating.

3D graphics and animation.

Support for touch and stylus input.

Example:

Code snippet

```
<Window x:Class="WpfApp.MainWindow"

xmlns="http://schemas.microsoft.com/winfx/20
06/xaml/presentation"
```

```
xmlns:x="http://schemas.microsoft.com/winfx/
2006/xaml"[3]
            Title="MainWindow" Height="350"
Width="525">
    <Grid>
            <Button Content="Click Me"
Click="Button_Click" />
    </Grid>[4]
</Window>
```

C#

```
using System.Windows;

namespace WpfApp
{
    public partial class MainWindow : Window
    {
        public MainWindow()
        {
            InitializeComponent();[5]
        }

            private void Button_Click(object
sender, RoutedEventArgs e)
        {
```

```
                    MessageBox.Show("Hello, WPF!");
                }
            }
        }
```

Choosing Between Windows Forms and WPF:

Windows Forms: Simple, rapid development for traditional desktop applications.

WPF: Complex, visually rich applications with advanced UI features.

Consider the following factors when making your choice:

Complexity of the UI: For simple UIs, Windows Forms may be sufficient. For complex UIs with advanced features, WPF is a better choice.

Performance: WPF can offer better performance, especially for complex graphics and animations.

Developer Experience: If you're familiar with traditional Windows Forms development, you may find it easier to get started with Windows Forms. However, if you're comfortable with XAML and modern UI development techniques, WPF is a good choice.

By understanding the strengths and weaknesses of Windows Forms and WPF, you can choose the right framework for your specific project needs.

Chapter 9

Web Development with ASP.NET Core

9.1 MVC Architecture

MVC stands for **Model-View-Controller**. It's a popular architectural pattern used to design user interfaces. It separates an application into three interconnected parts:

Model

Represents the data and business logic of the application.

Stores data and defines the rules for manipulating that data.

Independent of the user interface and the way data is presented.

View

Responsible for the visual representation of the data.

Defines the user interface elements like forms, buttons, and labels.

Displays the data retrieved from the Model.

Controller

Handles user input and updates the Model and View accordingly.

Receives user input, processes it, and updates the Model.

Instructs the View to update itself based on the changes in the Model.

How MVC Works

User Interaction: A user interacts with the View (e.g., clicks a button).

Controller Action: The Controller receives the user input and processes it.

Model Update: The Controller updates the Model with the new data.

View Update: The Model notifies the View about the changes.

View Rendering: The View retrieves the updated data from the Model and renders it to the user.

Advantages of MVC

Improved Code Organization: Clear separation of concerns.

Enhanced Testability: Easier to test individual components.

Reusability: Views and Models can be reused in different contexts.

Scalability: Easier to scale and maintain as the application grows.

Example (ASP.NET MVC):

Model: A C# class representing a product (e.g., Product.cs).

View: An ASP.NET Razor view (.cshtml) displaying product information.

Controller: A C# class handling user requests and interacting with the Model and View (e.g., ProductController.cs).

Real-world Applications of MVC:

Web applications (ASP.NET MVC, Ruby on Rails, Django)

Desktop applications (WPF)

Mobile applications (Angular, React Native)

By understanding the MVC pattern, you can create well-structured, maintainable, and scalable applications.

9.2 Razor Pages and Web API

Razor Pages

Razor Pages is a simplified approach to building web UI within ASP.NET Core. It combines the simplicity of ASP.NET Web Pages with the power of ASP.NET Core MVC.

Key Features:

Simplified Page-Based Model: Each page is a self-contained unit, combining the view and controller logic.

Razor Syntax: A concise syntax for embedding C# code within HTML.

Model Binding: Automatic binding of form data to model properties.

Tag Helpers: Custom HTML elements that simplify common tasks.

Routing: Flexible routing options for clean URLs.

Example:

Razor CSHTML

```
@page
@model IndexModel

<h1>Hello, @Model.Message</h1>
```

C#

```
public class IndexModel : PageModel
{
    public string Message { get; set; }

    public void OnGet()
    {
        Message = "World";
    }
}
```

Web API

ASP.NET Web API is a framework for building HTTP-based web APIs. It allows you to create RESTful services that can be consumed by various clients, such as web applications, mobile apps, and other services.

Key Features:

RESTful API Design: Supports HTTP methods like GET, POST, PUT, and DELETE.

Model Binding: Automatic binding of request data to model objects.

Routing: Flexible routing options for defining API endpoints.

Content Negotiation: Supports different content formats (JSON, XML, etc.).

Authentication and Authorization: Built-in support for authentication and authorization mechanisms.

Example:

C#

```
[ApiController]
[Route("[controller]")]
public class ProductsController : ControllerBase
{
    [HttpGet]
    public IEnumerable<Product> Get()
    {
        return[1] new Product[]
        {
            new Product { Id = 1, Name = "Product
1" },
            new Product { Id = 2, Name = "Product
2" }
        };
    }
}
```

Choosing Between Razor Pages and Web API:

Razor Pages: Ideal for building simple, page-based web applications.

Web API: Best for creating reusable, scalable, and API-driven services.

In many cases, you can combine Razor Pages and Web API to build robust web applications. Razor Pages can handle the user interface and routing, while Web API can provide data and services to the frontend.

Chapter 10

Building Real-World Applications

10.1 Console Applications

Console Applications in C#

A console application is a type of computer program that interacts with the user through a text-only interface, typically a command-line window. In C#, you can create console applications to perform various tasks, from simple calculations to complex data processing.

Basic Structure:

C#

```
using System;

namespace MyConsoleApp
{
    class Program
    {
        static void Main(string[] args)
        {
            Console.WriteLine("Hello, World!");
        }
    }
}
```

Key Components:

`using System;`: Imports the `System` namespace, which provides fundamental classes like `Console`, `Math`, and `IO`.

`namespace MyConsoleApp`: Declares a namespace to organize your code.

`class Program`: Defines a class named `Program`.

`static void Main(string[] args)`: The entry point of the application.

`static`: The method is accessible without creating an instance of the class.

`void`: The method doesn't return a value.

`Main`: The name of the method, which is the starting point.

`string[] args`: An array of strings that can be used to pass command-line arguments to the application.

`Console.WriteLine("Hello, World!");`: Writes the message "Hello, World!" to the console.

Input and Output:

Reading Input:

C#

```
string name = Console.ReadLine();
int age = int.Parse(Console.ReadLine());
```

Writing Output:

C#

```
Console.WriteLine("Your name is: " + name);
Console.Write("Your age is: ");
Console.WriteLine(age);
```

Example: A Simple Calculator

C#

```
using System;

namespace Calculator
{
    class Program
    {
        static void Main(string[] args)
```

```
        {
            Console.Write("Enter the first number: ");
            double[1] num1 = double.Parse(Console.ReadLine());

            Console.Write("Enter the second number: ");
            double num2 = double.Parse(Console.ReadLine());[2]

            Console.WriteLine("Sum: " + (num1 + num2));
            Console.WriteLine("Difference: " + (num1 - num2));
            Console.WriteLine("Product: " + (num1 * num2));
            Console.WriteLine("Quotient: " + (num1 / num2));[3]
        }
    }
}
```

Key Points:

Console applications are often used for simple scripts, tools, and command-line interfaces.

They can be compiled into executable files.

For more complex applications, consider using a graphical user interface (GUI) framework like Windows Forms or WPF.

Always handle potential exceptions, such as invalid input or file operations, to make your application more robust.

10.2 Windows Forms Applications

Windows Forms Applications

Windows Forms is a framework for building Windows desktop applications. It provides a rich set of controls, such as buttons, text boxes, and data grids, to create user interfaces.

Key Features:

Drag-and-Drop Interface Design: You can visually design your forms using a designer.

Event-Driven Programming: Respond to user actions by handling events like button clicks and form closing.

Rich Controls: A variety of controls for creating complex user interfaces.

Data Binding: Easily bind data to controls.

Deployment: Create standalone executable applications.

Basic Steps to Create a Windows Forms Application:

Create a New Project: In Visual Studio, create a new Windows Forms Application project.

Design the Form: Use the designer to add controls, set properties, and arrange layout.

Write Event Handlers: Double-click on controls to create event handlers and write code to respond to user actions.

Add Functionality: Implement the logic for your application, such as calculations, database operations, or file I/O.

Test and Debug: Run your application to test its functionality and fix any errors.

Deploy: Create a setup package to distribute your application.

Example: Simple Calculator

C#

```
using System;
using System.Windows.Forms;

namespace WindowsFormsApp1
{
    public partial class Form1 : Form
    {
        public Form1()
        {
            InitializeComponent();
        }

        private[1] void button1_Click(object sender, EventArgs e)
        {
            double num1 = double.Parse(textBox1.Text);
            double num2 = double.Parse(textBox2.Text);
            double result = num1 + num2;[2]
            label1.Text = result.ToString();
```

```
        }
    }
}
```

Advantages of Windows Forms:

Rapid Development: Visual designer and drag-and-drop capabilities.

Wide Range of Controls: Built-in controls for various UI elements.

Easy to Learn: Simple programming model for beginners.

Cross-Platform Compatibility: With .NET Core, Windows Forms applications can be deployed to multiple platforms.

Limitations of Windows Forms:

Less Flexible UI: Compared to WPF, Windows Forms may have limitations in terms of advanced UI features and customization.

Performance: For complex applications, WPF might offer better performance.

By understanding the basics of Windows Forms, you can create a wide range of desktop applications, from simple tools to complex business systems.

10.3 WPF Applications

Windows Presentation Foundation (WPF)

WPF is a powerful framework for building rich user interfaces in Windows applications. It offers a flexible and declarative approach to designing and developing user interfaces.

Key Features:

XAML: A declarative language for defining the UI layout and appearance.

Data Binding: Easily bind data to UI elements.

Styles and Templates: Create reusable UI elements and styles.

3D Graphics and Animation: Build visually stunning applications with 3D graphics and animations.

Document Model: Treat UI elements as documents, enabling advanced layout and formatting.

Basic Structure of a WPF Application:

XAML: Defines the visual structure of the application.

Code-Behind: Contains the C# code that handles events and logic.

Example:

XAML:

XML

```
<Window x:Class="WpfApp.MainWindow"

xmlns="http://schemas.microsoft.com/winfx/2006/xaml/presentation"

xmlns:x="http://schemas.microsoft.com/winfx/2006/xaml"[1]
                        Title="MainWindow"  Height="350"
Width="525">
     <Grid>
```

```
                    <Button Content="Click Me"
Click="Button_Click" />
    </Grid>[2]
</Window>
```

C# Code-Behind:

C#

```
using System.Windows;

namespace WpfApp
{
    public partial class MainWindow : Window
    {
        public MainWindow()
        {
            InitializeComponent();[3]
        }

        private void Button_Click(object sender,
RoutedEventArgs e)
        {
            MessageBox.Show("Hello, WPF!");
        }
    }
}
```

Advantages of WPF:

Rich User Interface: Create visually stunning applications with advanced UI features.

Data Binding: Easily bind data to UI elements.

Styling and Templating: Customize the appearance of controls.

3D Graphics and Animation: Leverage powerful graphics capabilities.

Modern UI: Supports touch, stylus, and other modern input methods.

Disadvantages of WPF:

Steeper Learning Curve: More complex than Windows Forms.

Performance Overhead: Can be resource-intensive for complex applications.

When to Use WPF:

When you need to create visually stunning applications with advanced UI features.

When you need to build data-driven applications with complex data binding scenarios.

When you want to leverage the power of 3D graphics and animation.

By mastering WPF, you can create sophisticated and engaging Windows applications.

www.ingramcontent.com/pod-product-compliance
Lightning Source LLC
Chambersburg PA
CBHW071109240526
45469CB00006BD/2395
9798302218919